ROCK YOUR TO-DO LIST:

GETTING TO YOUR BIGGEST GOALS FASTER, WITH LESS STRESS, IN ONLY 15 MINUTES A DAY

By Lain Ehmann, MPA

DEDICATION

To Kinsey Fay – the most organized teenager I know.
I love you, Booboo, always and forever.

TABLE OF CONTENTS

BONUS RESOURCES

Before you start, you may want to check out the bonus resources I've created for you, including worksheets, a screensaver, videos, and more. Just go over to http://www.lainehmann.com/rytdlextras and grab them there! And check back regularly, as I'll be adding more resources regularly.

INTRODUCTION

As a life and business coach, my goal is to help you get your deepest and most valued dreams out of your head and onto your to-do list. This is interactive, so I'm going to be giving you assignments along the way. Grab a pen and paper right now so you are ready to take notes. Even though I can't see you, just like Santa, I know when you've been good or bad. So let's just make it easy on ourselves, and when I ask a question, you just go right ahead and answer, just like I could hear you. Because I can. ;)

In this book, I'll be presenting a bunch of different topics as they relate to your to-do list. We'll be talking about big ideas like priorities and goals, and small ideas that may seem so simple that you wonder how in the heck they're going to help. You might, at times, think I'm a little bit loony. Well, I am! But I've also helped dozens of people, just like you, gain control over their schedules and lives. I can help you, too.

Some of the ideas I present will go 180 degrees against everything you've learned about productivity. Some of what I say might make you a bit mad or irritated, or make you say, "Well, if she only knew about MY life... this will never work for me!" But before you toss this book in the recycling bin or give it to the parakeet to use for training purposes, I want to challenge you. Give the Rock Your To-Do List process two weeks. Read through this book, incorporate and adopt the principles and actions I share, and put them to use. In two weeks' time if you have not significantly lowered your stress level and increased your productivity, you can go back to the old way of doing things.

While these ideas and principles will work in the office or workplace, or for someone who works for pay from home, the Rock Your To-Do

List program is designed to help you accomplish those "other" tasks and projects – from redoing the basement to starting a new business or getting back in shape. Many of the examples I present come from my own life, one without the strict boundaries of office work hours. If you do work outside the home for pay, you can easily apply the RYTDL process to your work life. I would suggest separating the two – having one list for "work" and one for "home."

Why? Because I find that, by and large, we are really good at getting stuff done for OTHER people, but we're not so great about getting it done when it's "just" for us. In other words, it's really common to be the most productive, detail-oriented, goal-driven person in the office, but at home you just can't seem to get on the treadmill or tackle the pile of receipts and bank statements to get your personal taxes in order. So while I'll be focusing on non-employee productivity, know that this process will work for your office hours, too.

Imagine yourself waking up every morning feeling in control. You are confident about the day, knowing exactly what you need to accomplish, and knowing you can accomplish it. We will also have the security of knowing you are attacking your highest and best goals, one day at a time.

What have you got to lose?

CH. 1: YOU ARE NOT THE PROBLEM: MY STORY

There are tons of books on productivity and goal-setting available. You can spend as little as $.99 or as much as $1500 or more for a three-day seminar with a guru. But even after spending hours of my own life testing out everything from David Allen's "Getting Things Done" to the Franklin-Covey method, I still saw plenty of gaps in the process.

At first, I felt like I was the problem. After all, these were well-paid, well-established experts in the field of productivity. Who was I to tell them their programs didn't work? So I limped along, trying to put my daily to-do list into little boxes, or arrange the items according to an arcane priority system, or to choose my "One Thing" and focus solely on that (problem: the remaining two kids and my husband didn't appreciate it much when it wasn't THEIR day and I told them they had to fend for themselves!).

Sometimes I thought it was just the nuts and bolts of what I was using. The Dayplanner wasn't working, so I invested in a leather Filofax. But I could only afford the smallest version, and that wasn't large enough to contain all my various projects, ideas, schedules, and notes, so I upgraded to the Franklin Planner. I nearly threw out my shoulder toting that bad boy around with me, so it had to go as well. I've tried Day Design calendars, Month-at-a-Glance, Week-at-a-Glance, Daytimers, Day Runners, and everything in between.

But I always came to the same results; first, that copying my calendar from one planner to the next might seem productive, but it really did nothing to get me more hours in my day. Second, the systems as they were presented to me just weren't working.

Finally, one day I thought, "What if the problem isn't ME? What if the problem is the system?"

Now, I'm pretty much trained to think that if something is going wrong, it's my fault. After all, I'm not only a Type A personality, I'm an eldest daughter and the mom of three AND a recovering perfectionistic people-pleaser. So the idea that I WASN'T the issue was, well, revolutionary.

I sat with that concept for a while, and eventually felt a great sense of peace wash over me. It wasn't that I was having problems choosing my "One Thing;" it was that in my world of kids and jobs and husbands and dogs and never-ending household chores, there WASN'T a "One Thing."

The fact that I broke out in an anger rash when I was forced to decide if something was an A-3 or a B-1 task didn't reveal some deep psychological issue about my inner state; it simply meant that the time spent assigning priorities was sucking up the only free time I had in my schedule, so it's no wonder I resented it!

And that I wasn't a bad person, even though I couldn't seem to follow the advice to simply close my office door to focus on my Number One priority "until it was done" (partly because I don't have an office; partly because I was always being interrupted by Those Darned Kids and That Darned Husband and the phone and the neighbor and the laundry and for the love of all that's holy, emails from real-live CUSTOMERS and CLIENTS who had some crazy idea that giving me money meant that I needed to answer their questions in a timely manner).

When I packed away all the time-management books (except a few, which I'll get to) and sat down with a blank monthly calendar, my to-do list, and a notebook, I soon realized that anything I was accomplishing was IN SPITE OF the advice in these books, not because of them.

As they say in Boston, "Light dawns on Marblehead[1]!"

Then I took a look at the books and gurus and programs and realized that virtually ALL OF THEM were written by men. Men with office doors. Men with staff and employees and assistants. Men with wives who would deal with the kid stuff and the home stuff so they, in exchange, could actually close said office door and focus on that number-one priority.

Now, I'm not big on stereotypes and generalities (I'm that kid in class who would always, always think of the one exception to the rule). But I do know from an informal survey of my clients, friends, and family that women, whether they're working in the home, outside the home, or both, tend to have more projects they're juggling at once than men do.

If you are a man who is able to juggle Pirate Day at preschool with the need to provide a no-peanut, no-gluten snack for the soccer team and a client meeting and an appointment to get your roots taken care of, more power to you. Read on; you will love this book. But if you are one of those types who thinks multi-tasking should be outlawed and you've never dropped your phone in the toilet in the Target restroom because you were trying to pull up the three-year-old's tights while balancing a diaper bag on your knee AND talk to your boss about next week's sales meeting, then you probably aren't going to find much here. Move along, yo. Go see David Allen or Leo Babauta. You'll love them.

Now that I've alienated half the readers, let's get down to business.

After rejecting most of the information I learned in the programs I'd spent hours upon hours studying and modeling (yeah, you're welcome), I struck out on my own. I had been winging it for several years as I raised kids, drove carpools, moved across the country

---

1   I have no idea where this saying comes from. I take it to mean that someone who was acting dense (like a "marblehead") suddenly "sees the light."

and back again, ran half-marathons, cooked meals, and built online businesses. I seemed to be getting a lot done – more than most people. And when I finally realized that I was getting more questions about my planning and goal-setting than I was about my new haircut or cute shoes, I knew I had something women needed to learn.

So I started deconstructing my process, figuring out what worked, what didn't and why, and then slicing and dicing my knowledge and experiences into a Frankenstein-esque program that I christened "Rock Your To-Do List" (mainly because it sounds better than "The Frankenstein" or, my second choice, "Nothing Else Worked.")

Here are the truths upon which RYTDL and this book were designed:

1. **No two schedules are the same because no two lives are the same.** We have different expectations, different goals, different priorities, and different personalities. Many time-management programs don't take that fact into consideration. As a result, those programs don't work for everyone because if you don't fit their one-size-fits-all mold, you're left like I was the first time I went into an American Apparel store and tried on a skirt: With your belly exposed on one end and your rear hanging out on the other. Not attractive.

2. **Women's lives are different than men's lives.** As stated above, you may be the exception to the rule, but in general, women have more projects and competing priorities than men do. I'm writing for an audience of people who know why I laugh when I read about the evils of multi-tasking. Sure, it would be great to only have one thing to think about at a time, but I gave up single-focus way back in 4th grade when I finally outgrew my Shaun Cassidy crush.

3. **Prescriptive programs don't work.** I'm going to teach you a PROCESS for moving towards your goals and ensuring

that tomorrow's dreams end up on today's schedule. But there aren't going to be a ton of flat directives, like "always do your housework before lunch," or, "get dressed 'to shoes' first thing in the morning," or "never leave your bed unmade." Those rules might work for some people, but they also just become another way for us to focus on the details rather than on the bigger picture. Heck, if you are spending your spare time inventing a product that will help me lose weight while watching Netflix and eating Doritos, I don't care if you ever make your bed again! Priorities, folks. Priorities.

4. **Life needs to be enjoyable.** You know those financial programs that suggest you give up eating out, lattes, manicures, new clothing, and haircuts that cost more than $5 for the next 50 years so you can retire without having to move in with your kids or eat cat food in your old age? Well, I don't know about you, but when I read that advice, I immediately call over my shoulder to whichever kid is within earshot, "Get my room ready, sonny boy, because I'm moving in!" Ten years of relative comfort in exchange for 40 years of pure monastic lifestyle doesn't seem like much of a deal to me. My goal is to help you find a way that lets you live your life NOW without having to get up at 3 in the morning to work on your novel or go to the gym, and without canceling your Netflix account. You CAN have your Downton Abbey and eat it, too... or something like that.

5. **Simple doesn't mean easy.** I'm going to present to you a process that you will, at times, think about and say, "Really? How did I not figure this out myself?" You may think I'm nuts or a scam artist because it seems TOO simple. But trust me, if it were easy, you'd already be doing it. And sometimes it takes someone to connect the dots for you, in order to show you the picture that was there all along. Don't get fooled into

thinking you can skip steps or ignore my hard-won advice; you'll do so at your own peril. And I am EXACTLY the type of person who, when you come to me later and say, "Lain, I totally should have listened to you," will undoubtedly turn to you with a superior lift of the eyebrow and say, "I told you so." I may even say it two or three times. Hey, it's a cheap thrill! So save us the effort and just listen to me now.

My goal is to teach you some very specific ideas as to how you are going to change the way you are using your to-do list and your daily planning in order to move forward towards your dreams. I want you to have tools at your disposal to use over and over again so you can have your to-do list reflect your most precious goals. I want you to get those goals out of DREAM state and get them into TODAY state.

A major part of the RYTDL process is starting with the big picture and working backwards from there. So often we get absorbed with the minutiae of the everyday and forget to take a look at the 1000-foot-view. We're consumed with the dog's vet appointment and the overdue library books and the meals that need to be made and the work meetings, and so we forget to make sure what we are doing TODAY is moving us in the direction of where we want to be TOMORROW, NEXT MONTH, NEXT YEAR.

What I DO NOT want to have happen is for you to close this book and say, "Well, that was some great information but I don't know what to do next or how to apply that to my everyday life." I want you to leave me totally pumped and inspired, and ready for tomorrow. If that isn't where you are at the end of our time together, you need to speak up. Email me, contact me on Facebook, or send a smoke signal (I do live in Arizona, after all).

Sound good? Then let's get this show on the road. Time's a-wastin'.

YOUR ASSIGNMENT: Write down the various calendars, programs, processes, and systems you've attempted to follow. What were the drawbacks? What worked and what didn't? Where did you feel frustration? Keep these thoughts and discoveries in mind as you move forward through the rest of this book. Knowing where your own stumbling blocks are will help you adjust the RYDL program to work for YOU.

CH. 2: WHAT'S YOUR DAMAGE?

Back in the 80s in California, when someone was being peevy or just plain out of sorts, we'd say, "What's your damage?" Of course, we said it with a Moon Zappa-worthy Valley Girl sneer. (We thought we were much cooler than we were. Heck, my kids still tell me I think I'm much cooler than I actually am. Maybe it's because I'm still listening to Moon Zappa and saying things like, "What's your damage?" and "Gag me with a spoon!")

Spoons aside, when you look at your daily productivity or list, where are the pain points? There's something going on in your life that made you pick up this book. Is it lack of motivation to tackle things on your daily list? Is it lack of direction? Is too much to do with not enough time? Or a little bit (or a lot!) of all of the above?

Where are you, right now? Tell me as specifically as you can what your issue is and, on a scale of one to five, how painful that is.

Maybe you wake up every morning (if you've managed to sleep at all), full of dread, just thinking about the day ahead and all the stuff you just aren't going to have time to do. Your pain might be 4 or 5.

Or maybe you have a handle on your everyday schedule but you are running yourself ragged to get it all done. You'd like to bring more focus to your days. You might be at a 2 or 3.

Or maybe you aren't sure you are heading in the right direction, and you want to make sure your life is headed towards your deepest priorities. You might be at a 2.

Whatever the number, make note of it. It's important to know what we're working with – and what we're working on – so we know why we're even reading this book full of '80s pop references and bad jokes in the first place.

Using this scale:

5 – It's keeping you up at night

1 – No big deal

Where are you? Make note of that number. It doesn't define you, but it does control a portion of your life. Now get ready, because we're about to reclaim that time and energy.

CH. 3: YOU DON'T NEED TO DO MORE

I've got some good news for you.

I'm not into pain. In fact, I tried to read "50 Shades of Grey," but the first time I picked it up I got a paper cut and that was it for me.

Bad joke, I know. But if you were worried that I was going to tell you that you need to get up with the roosters, or skip your weekly movie night with the family, or give up Words with Friends, in order to stay on top of your to-do list, I'm not going in that direction. Instead, I'm going to help you go through a filtering process to help you take things OFF your list to make room for the items that are most critical to your long-term goals.

The reason for this is two-fold.

First, drastic change is not sustainable. I'm sure you've seen or at least heard of "The Biggest Loser," where overweight people are whisked away from their everyday sedentary lives of Doritos and couch-potatoing, and taken to a hidden location where they're forced by mean trainers to work out for like 26 hours a day and live on celery sticks and water. They lose enormous amounts of weight and have a big "reveal," but then within a few months of returning to their everyday lives, they find the weight creeping back on. It's because they don't have the ability to stick with a 500-calorie-a-day diet forever and ever. It's simply not sustainable.

Bring this knowledge to our to-do list makeover; sure, you may be able to get up two hours early for a month or two, but then daylight savings comes or the kids get out of school or you take a vacation and suddenly you're right back into the slovenly life of sleeping in until (gasp!) 7 o'clock. And all the hard work you accomplished goes right out the window. And then you beat yourself up, reaffirming your failure, and you're right back where you started, but worse because now you're doubting your ability to make any kind of positive change at all. Not good.

Whatever adjustments you make, I want them to be life-long habits that you build into your routine. I don't want you to slip back to the "old" way just because I'm not standing over you with a stopwatch and half a non-fat rice cake as a reward.

The second reason for avoiding pain is that it's no fun. I want you to enjoy your life. I want you to think I walk on water. I want you to be so happy and positive about this whole RYTDL experience that you write to Pope Francis and ask him to canonize me (except while I'm alive, please). While it's great to accomplish big goals, most of our life is spent IN PROCESS, rather than at the finish line.

Recently, I decided it would be a good thing to run a half-marathon. Yeah, I know. Pain. But still, I'd had one or two too many celebratory margaritas on New Year's Eve and ended up signing up for a 13-mile race (it's actually 13.1 miles, but I figure I'll be crawling that last 1/10th mile, so I'm not counting it).

The .05 seconds I'll spend crossing the finish line is an infinitesimal part of the entire race. And it's an even smaller part of the overall training process. So while I know that I'll enjoy that point in time, it's even more important to enjoy the two and a half hours leading up to the finish line moment – not to mention the three months I've spent training for the big day!

So whatever I ask you to do, I want you to think about doing it for the long haul, not for a sprint of a few weeks or months. I want to change your life, not change the five weeks between seasons of "Dancing with the Stars." It's something for your lifetime, not for your summer vacation.

So if I'm not going to be asking you to burn the candle at both ends, you might be wondering how you're ever going to start crossing things off your bucket – or like I call it, life – list. Here's the secret: It's not about doing more. It's about doing the RIGHT things.

Way back in the 1900s, an Italian economist named Vilfredo Pareto discovered that 80 percent of the land in Italy at the time was owned by just 20 percent of the population. He then studied other countries' land distribution, with a similar result. He then extrapolated his concept to other populations and measurable elements, and this rule of thumb was born: That 80 percent of the effects come from 20 percent of the causes.

If you are a real estate agent, it means that 80 percent of your income will be generated by 20 percent of your clients.

If you are a software developer, it means that 80 percent of the complaints can be fixed by addressing 20 percent of the bugs in the program.

If you are a parent, it means that 80 percent of the squabbles in your family are caused by 20 percent of the kids. :)

And when it comes to our to-do lists, it means that 80 percent of the value of the list lies in only 20 percent of the items. Stated another way, if you have a list of 10 tasks, the biggest bang will come from only two (2!!!) items on your list.

Now, this rule is not absolute. Sometimes it's a bit more, and sometimes it's a bit less. But the critical thing to remember is that not all of the tasks on your list are created equal. Some are going to move you way forward towards your ultimate dreams and goals, while others are simply rearranging the deck chairs on the Titanic; it may make things look better, but you're not keeping the ship from hitting the iceberg.

You, being the smart and analytical person I know you to be, are probably wondering about now... "Lain, that's all well and good. But how do I know WHICH two items are going to make a difference in my life?"

Good question! (You are so smart!)

The answer is, look over your list.

- Which items have gotten moved from day to day to day?

- Which items strike fear in your heart and butterflies in your stomach?

- Which items constantly get moved down the list in favor of the day-to-day grind?

THOSE are the ones you need to do to move forward to your goals.

For some crazy, ironic reason, the critical 20 percent is almost always the tasks that get pushed off to the next day or never get done at all. Those things that are important are sacrificed at the altar of the urgent – going to the store, making dinner, running errands. And though those things may be hanging over your head and need to get done to keep your life functioning, they aren't the ones that move you toward your highest and best goals.

So the question becomes, how do we make sure we make time for those things that are most critical to us to ensure we meet our goals? The key is to do LESS. I'm going to show you how to filter your to-do list, removing items and re-prioritizing others. What's left will be the things that you (and only you!) need to do, today. What's left will be the things that will make a difference in your life, not just because you'll have clean socks in your drawer, but because you'll be making progress toward the future you've always wanted.

I'll be honest: You may have to stay up a bit later, or get up a tiny bit earlier, but it's not going to be painful, I promise. You're going to learn how to enjoy your life today while working towards tomorrow.

YOUR ASSIGNMENT: Have you ever started an all-in exercise, fitness, or other regimen? How did it work for you? If you were successful during the program, were you able to maintain your results after the program ended?

CH. 4: THE POWER OF THE LIST

With the kajillion options out there in the world, from fancy iPhone apps to calendar systems and beyond, I have never found something as flexible, powerful, and effective as a simple written to-do list.

There are four main reasons to create a to-do list:

First, it serves as a reinforcement of my highest and best use of my time.

Sure, it's a list of the stuff I need to get done… But it goes beyond that. By writing down my daily priorities in a certain manner, I am constantly filtering each opportunity presented to me throughout my day through a very powerful lens: the lens of my dreams. In my experience from working with dozens upon dozens of clients one-on-one, and in groups and workshops, we spend very little time thinking about our dreams.

Yes, we think about the future: how we're going to pay for college, what we need to pick up at the grocery store for meals in the coming week, or whether it's time to replace our oil filter. But we don't think about our brightest future. We are so concerned about the now and what's going to happen tomorrow and next week, that the big stuff gets put on hold. Of course, the problem with that is that we never seem to get to it. A to-do list, when prepared and used in the way I'll teach you, will bring those bright secret golden dreams out of the shoebox in the closet and into the light, and even into today. You're going to be totally jazzed when you see how easy it is to start building that future you've always dreamed about.

Second, people get distracted. There are millions upon millions of calls for our attention each and every day. Having a concrete reminder of your focus for the next 24 hours pulls you back home again and again. There's no excuse for not writing the next chapter in your book because you "forgot." It was right there in front of you, hopefully something you looked at several times over the course of the day.

Third, a to-do list is a black-and-white (sometimes literally) assessment of whether or not you are getting the right things done. When your to-do list is created correctly, at the end of the day it serves as a scorecard for the previous 24 hours. So often we go through life with no feedback. Are we being a good mom? A good employee? A good business owner? A good human? It's hard to tell.

But when you have your to do list to go by and those checks or strikethroughs marking off the things you've completed, you can pat yourself on the back and rest your head on the pillow knowing that you did what you were supposed to do. (Secret: don't tell, but I sometimes go back and look through old to do lists just as a way to encourage myself and let myself know I'm not just taking up oxygen on this planet. I'm actually getting big stuff done – and I have proof!)

The fourth reason might be the most important to you. Quite simply, to-do lists work. If you follow my process for creating and using your own personal to-do list, you will get more done than you ever thought possible. You'll be focused, productive, and effective, the most powerful trio since Crosby, Stills and Nash cut their last album.

YOUR ASSIGNMENT: Do you currently keep a written to-do list? Is it on your phone or computer, or on paper? How do you use it? Is it successful?

CH. 5: LET'S GET CLEAR

Up until this point, I've been throwing around the term "to-do list," setting aside for the moment the idea that what *I* call a to-do list may not be the same thing you're referring to. I did that purposely; I wanted to share some grounding principles first before we started discussing definitions.

And now is the time to dive in and get clear on this very important term.

You might be thinking that of course you know what a to-do list is. After all, the answer is the question: A to-do list is a list of, you got it, things you need to do.

But.

But there's more to it than that.

With something as simple as a written to do list, you might think we can just jump right in. But don't let its simplicity fool you. You may have had this experience yourself: you sit down with a sheet of paper or a computer file and you start to spew. You write down everything you need to do for the next, oh, three years or so. Buy a birthday present for Aunt Marge? Check. Graduate from law school? Check. Feed the dog? Check. It's all there.

Half an hour later, you are feeling pretty good. You just know you are on your way to organization and completion.

But somehow, looking at that list of 473 items is not inspiring. Where do you start? Law school or Rover who's begging at your feet? (Guess contract law is going to have to wait.)

And what about the new things you have to add as you move through your day? Do they just go to the bottom of the list, or do you slot them in between other items? Should you group them together by category or priority, or alphabetically, or in order of what you want to do most or least? So many choices!

Pretty soon, the list outlives its usefulness. It gets scratched up and scratched out, it's hard to read, and the undone items are just mocking you. So the list gets recycled, tucked into a back drawer, or forgotten in the lost file on your MacBook Pro. You chalk this to-do list stuff off just to another crazy idea that won't work for you.

So what's going to be different this time? In a word: everything. To-do lists don't work if they're just a collection of random thoughts and ideas from your brain. Instead, they need to be carefully cultivated and intentional, and cover a specific period of time. Also, as we've discussed, they are most effective when they reflect your deepest and most cherished goals and dreams. You know, the stuff that keeps you up at night and that you dream about in dead time.

At first glance, you might think that this is a stupid question. But what is a to-do list?

Umm, duh.

Sure, it is a list of tasks you have to do. But here's where it gets tricky, and exciting.

A to-do list is not your grocery list.

A to-do list is not your bucket list.

A to-do list is not a brain dump of every project, task, and unfinished idea that gallops through your brain.

A to-do list is not a mental accounting of errands you must run and phone calls to return.

Okay, then… What is it?

Here's how I define it: A to-do list is a short, targeted, written list of tasks to complete today in order to accomplish your biggest goals.

Let's hit some of those high points:

A To-Do List Is Short. We've all had the experience of looking at a list that is a page or 20 long, and wondering how the heck we were going to get it all done. Writing down more than you can possibly accomplish in any given 24 hours is counterproductive. Just adding a kajillion and one items to your to-do list does not count towards some cosmic good girl list. If you write more than you can accomplish in the next 24 hours, you are just distracting yourself, fooling yourself, and giving yourself an excuse for not getting the important stuff done.

Some productivity experts will recommend you limit your important tasks to three or so, but I don't think that's realistic. Also, the most important thing you do today might only take 30 seconds. What are you going to do with the other 23 hours and 59 ½ minutes of your day? I mean, there are only so many back episodes of "Scandal" that one person can watch straight before going into a coma!

At the same time, though, you **must** limit the things on your list to tasks you could reasonably expect to complete in one day.

I know… This is where you raise your hand and say, "But Lain! I have so much to do! I have more to do than any 10 Grinches could finish in a day! I can't leave those items off my list."

Yeah, you can. Just writing something on your list doesn't mean anything. You only get credit for stuff you actually finish. So if you're not going to get it done, why put it on your list in the first place?

This is my book, so we're playing by my rules. And I say, limit your list to things you would expect to realistically accomplish today. That doesn't mean there isn't a place for those other tasks and projects. It just means they do not belong on your little dated list for today. We will talk more about holding places for longer-term projects, ideas, and tasks. But suffice it to say, they do not belong on your list for today if you're not going to do them today.

But, but, but… You're spluttering. I've got so much to do. There's no way I can cut the stuff off my list! Well, let's get real. The reality is that you only have a certain number of hours in the day. And if you've been one of those people who consistently and habitually writes way more on your list than you could ever get done, you are going to bed at night with stuff undone. "How's that working for you?" as Dr. Phil would say. My guess is that you're setting your head on your pillow with a feeling of failure because it didn't all get done. And then you're waking up in the morning already feeling behind from the day before. What's the good in that?

It doesn't do you any good to create a to-do list with 57 items, 47 of which can't be completed in the next 24 hours. When you do that, your list just becomes a parking lot. And you know how you come out of the mall during the craziness of shopping the weekend before Christmas, and you can't find your car? That's what it's like when you have to many things on your to do list. You can't figure out where you are supposed to be going. You get all turned around, and you end up wandering around the parking lot in a daze, cutting from row to row with people giving you the fisheye cause they thought you were going to lead them to a soon to be vacated space.

My process asks that you make those tough decisions up front before you even create your to-do list for the day. Imagine waking up feeling in control and confident that the things assigned to you and that you've chosen to take on for the next 24 hours are actually accomplishable. Imagine checking 90 percent-plus of the items on your list off every day. How is that going to change your life? How are you going to feel at the end of each day?

That's power, my friend.

Now, let's move along.

A To-Do List Is Targeted. Did you know that a laser beam that can cut through steel or cement is really just a collection of photons? Yep, the same particles of light that gave you that golden tan you now regret spending hours cultivating in your teens, can slice through a refrigerator like a knife cutting through warm butter. How? It's the power of focus.

Lasers concentrate the light particles into such a dense mass that it can destroy virtually anything in its path.

You probably see where I'm going here, being the smarty pants that I know you are. The more targeted and focused you are, the more powerful you become.

You might be thinking that's fine and dandy for a collection of photons who don't have to drive their kids to hockey practice and take the dog in for his annual chakra realigning. How are you supposed to be focused when there are so many disparate calls for your attention and time?

Oh, scientists will tell you that it's not all that easy to condense photons into a powerful laser beam. And I will tell you it's also not easy to reclaim your focus again and again during your day. I'll be sharing some of my favorite strategies for maintaining my focus in future sections. Once you get the hang of asking and answering the critical questions, you'll be condensing your own personal photons like nobody's business.

A To-Do List Is Written. You are smart, we've ascertained that. But even the brightest of brains cannot keep everything in its proper cranial compartments. It's been said that Albert Einstein couldn't remember his own phone number! So if the inventor of modern physics couldn't keep everything straight, how can we possibly remember to call the kids' orthodontist to reschedule next Tuesday's appointment for the Thursday after? In the words of Thomas Dolby, our brains are like a sieve.

Instead of mourning the fact that our minds are not steel traps, we need to just work with it. And this fact can actually work in our favor. Numerous studies have shown that people who write down their goals have a much higher likelihood of achieving them than those who keep it all upstairs in the old mental attic.

Just the process of filtering through all the various items you could possibly do and choosing the few to commit to paper has an inspiring effect. There is a connection between your hand, your brain, and your eyes. Seeing it written in black-and-white makes it somehow more "official" than if it were just a mental list. There is also no wiggle room. It's either on your list, or it's not. It's either something you're supposed to do today, or it's not.

We can play a lot of tricks with our brains. We can easily convince ourselves that "schedule colonoscopy" wasn't really on the list for today, and instead we are supposed to "buy new shoes." Writing down your list keeps us from playing these kinds of mental gymnastics with ourselves.

And as much as I am a believer in the good old-fashioned pen and paper, I will make an allowance for those of you who have put both feet into the digital age. As long as your to-do list is in a written format, I'm not going to have a fit if it's on your iPhone, iPad, laptop, etc. It just needs to be all written down, and in a place you can access it whenever you need it.

And that last part is exactly why I prefer the paper to-do list. I can take it to the pool without fear of the kids splashing it with water. If I think of something to add while I'm driving down Tatum Boulevard driving my kids to school, I can quickly scrawl something on the notebook on the seat next to me without fear of ramming us all into a stop sign. So if your digital list is working for you, great. But if you think you can do better, take a page out of my book (pun intended) and write that sucker down.

YOUR ASSIGNMENT: It's time to commit to using a written to-do list for the next four weeks. Your assignment is to find a notebook that you can carry with you at all times to keep your list in. It doesn't have to be fancy – I often use a spiral notebook that fits in my tote bag or a Moleskine-type book. Find one you like, and get in the habit of carrying it with you.

CH. 6: AUDIT TIME

We've taken a look at how typical time-management programs fail us, and why it's not our fault. We've talked about what a to-do list is, and how it can help you achieve your biggest, most precious goals. We've also visited the idea of how making progress lies not in doing more, but in doing the right things. Now, I'd like to dive into your personal challenges with keeping a to-do list.

Answer the following questions with "Yes" or "No." If it's mostly yes, put down "Yes." Don't get hung up on the answer; just go with your gut. It's usually right!

1. I have more than 10 items on my to-do list.

2. I often move items from one day's list to the next.

3. There are items on my list that are more than a week old.

4. I don't have a written to-do list at all – I keep it all in my head!

5. I have items on my list that will take more than 15 minutes to complete.

6. I have items on my to-do list that aren't necessary to achieve my highest-priority goals.

7. I have items on my list that it's tough or impossible to "complete," like "Get in shape" or "Get organized." (i.e., they are projects rather than goals.)

8. I have mystery items on my to-do list that I can't remember writing down, or explain what they are, such as "J.D." or "cat."

9. I regularly rewrite my to-do list, hoping that somehow I'll end up more organized, or discover secret caches of time to get things done.

10. When I tackle my to-do list, I start with the most fun or easiest tasks first, leaving the tougher or unpleasant tasks for later in the day.

SCORING: Give yourself one point for each "Yes" or mostly yes answer. TOTAL: _____

0-3: To-Do List Master! There may be a few places where you can refine your approach to your daily tasks, but overall, you're getting it done and getting it done well.

4-7: Firefighter. You are flying by the seat of your pants, going from fire to fire. You work on whatever catches your fancy, or whatever is at the top of your email in-box. As a result, you are constantly trying to keep all your projects moving forward, and you often wonder if you're moving in the right direction. You're busy, but not necessarily productive.

8-10: Donkey on the Edge. You wake up every morning knowing you'll never get it all done, and you go to bed feeling like you've failed again. You're always behind, and you constantly have the feeling of letting others – and yourself – down. You want to do better, but you're not sure how.

YOUR ASSIGNMENT: Circle or make note of the category you fall into, but don't get too attached to it! I want you to return to this audit in a month or two to take it again and see where you are. Many people going through this process are able to reduce their score 2-3 points in a matter of a month or so.

If you fall into a category you don't like, it is okay. You're not going to stay there for long! This is just like your blood pressure – in and of itself, it doesn't necessarily mean anything. But tracking it over time, or using it in conjunction with other inputs, can give us a good sense of where we are and what we need to work on.

CH. 7: FIRST THINGS FIRST

Now that you know the power of the to-do list, you're probably raring to go jump into a makeover of your own list. But let's pull the camera back a bit before we go into the day-to-day. In order for our to-do lists to move us in the right direction, we have to know what the right direction is!

Look around where you are right now. Whether you're in your bedroom (like I am) or at the office or at the local Starbucks, you can probably see a million calls for your attention, right now. As I scan my bedroom, I see laundry that needs to be folded (always!), my daughter's computer and school books that need to be put away, a stack of books to read, and dogs to walk, hand weights to lift, and Facebook – always Facebook!

So how is it possible to know what the right things are at any point in time? Well, we have to start at the top; we start with our priorities – our dreams, our "grand visions," as I call them. We have to start with exactly what you want your future to look like, in Technicolor, complete with Dolby surround sound and 3D.

It's popular these days to select a word for the year, or create an intention like "beauty," "grace," or "fly." If you've fallen into this trend, it feels really good to pick a word that you want to represent your year. Maybe you get a necklace engraved, and you might paint it on your wall, and you excitedly tell others about what you're intending for the upcoming 12 months, but often that's where it ends.

After all, how do you bring "fly" or "breathe" out of the ether into the everyday? How do you make it something you can DO? It's difficult, which is why we often lose touch with our word (or our resolutions) somewhere around springtime.

But never fear. I have an alternative to the ephemeral. I'm going to help you create goals and dreams that are actually DO-ABLE, but first let's talk about priorities. You probably know by now that I'm a word nerd, so I like to start with the definition. According to Professor Google, a priority is:

A thing that is regarded as more important than another. The fact or condition of being regarded or treated as more important. The right to take precedence or to proceed before others.

I love that priorities are things that are TREATED as more important, not just things that we SAY are more important. [2]

When we start talking about priorities, the ones that come up most often are those I call "The Five Fs:"

- Faith

- Family

- Friends

- Fitness

- Finances

Other common values include community, creativity, leadership, relationships, authenticity, and more.

---

2   I discuss priorities extensively in my book "FOUND: Rediscovering Your Dreams, Your Voice, and Your Life in 15 Minutes a Day" (http://www.lainehmann. com/getfound). Please take a look at it if you'd like more discussion on how to choose your priorities and values.

These are all great words... but how do you take, say, "relationships," and put it on your to-do list? There's nothing to *do*, and as we've discussed, that's what a to-do list IS – things you can DO. And that right there is the big disconnect between dreams and intentions and the everyday.

We often know what we want in a fuzzy, feel-good, long-term sense, but we don't know what to do TODAY to get there. We have an intuitive sense of what our priorities or "one word" means, but we don't make sure we know *exactly* what we want. And if we get to the point where we can say that our priority is "relationships," we're still not sure where we're headed because, even though we know that "relationships" are important to us, there are a million different types of relationships. There are even a million types of GOOD relationships!

As a result, it becomes frustrating and difficult to work today towards this dream for tomorrow. So March or April comes and we set our dreams and intentions aside, and we go back to folding laundry and answering the stuff at the top of the email in-box. After all, there's plenty of that to keep us busy.

If you're tired of living that way, of trying hard but not making the progress you long to, then let's keep going. It's time to take the first step to rocking your to-do list by determining your priorities.

YOUR ASSIGNMENT: Take five minutes to write down your top three to five priorities. Don't worry about the order (if "health" comes before or after "faith," for instance). Don't worry about if you're getting them all down; this is just a starting point.

Don't worry if your priorities are different than they were a year or two ago. At different periods in our life things might move up and down the priority list. You are not static – your life changes, your priorities change. That's GOOD. Just think about right here and now, and what your priorities are today. This is just a snapshot in time, so don't let it stress you out. I'm teaching you a process, something you can go back to again and again.

Remember, there are no "right" or "wrong" priorities; they are uniquely yours and require no defense or explanation.

CH. 8: WHY PRIORITIES AREN'T ENOUGH

Priorities are a necessary, but not sufficient, step towards rocking your to-do list. Unfortunately, it's often where most people stop. They get a list of the things that they want and that are important to them, and then they move into the new year or new season all charged up with no plan whatsoever as to how to make those dreams come to fruition. And this is where resolutions fail. We know what matters to us, but that's not enough. We have to break them down into GOALS.

I wrote a blog post a while back about how I'm sick of resolutions. I'm sick of the one word trend. I'm sick of seeing people start out the year with all this confetti and celebration and then fall flat about April. It is depressing and demotivating, and it breaks my heart. I want people to LIVE THEIR GOALS, not just set them. I don't want people to fail – I want them to SOAR.

Unfortunately, that's not the norm. And writers and bloggers and motivational speakers and gurus are a big part of the problem! People get all fired up and set on their way, but there's no support. They're left on the edge of the path through the jungle with no plan as to how to move forward into their future. And that's why most people don't have the life they dream of – because they have no idea how to take it from HERE to THERE.

Here's the good news: I see the problem, and I know the path. I'm going to help you create your own path – and the first step is to turn those dreams into goals.

YOUR ASSIGNMENT: Have you had the experience of setting resolutions that fall flat because you don't know how to break them down into actionable goals? How did it make you feel? What would have helped you move forward to accomplishment?

CH. 9: GOAL IN ONE

oals are another term we throw around without fully
understanding what they are and how they differ from
priorities. Google tells us that goals are:

The object of a person's ambition or effort; an aim or desired result.

The part I want you to pay attention to is the last part: "desired result."
For instance, "HOME" is a great value, but it's not necessarily a result.
"FINANCES" is a great value, but it's not a result. So to take the
next step towards reaching the future we desire, we need to take those
large, fuzzy words and turn them into results.

Several issues pop up when we talk about setting goals:

Problem #1: We set goals that are vague. Let's say your priority
is FITNESS, and you choose a goal of "Getting in shape." But that
goal isn't defined enough to make it inspirational and actionable. For
instance, getting in shape means something very different to you than
it does to someone who's an Ironman triathlete trying to secure a place
in the Olympics, or to someone who's 80 and just wants to be able to
maintain mobility. We have to define the goal much more specifically
before we can use it to drive our to-do list. If we don't get specific,
then we fall into the same problem we talked about before; we have
ideas but no way to translate them into action today. This leads to
frustration and eventually, surrender.

Problem #2: We set goals we don't really care about. About five
years ago, I signed up for a super-intensive Bible study program
through our church called Bible Study Fellowship (BSF). If you're

familiar with it, you know it requires a weekly commitment to attend the study, in addition to several hours of homework per week. I was excited to participate mainly because a friend of mine was a BSF leader and I wanted to get to know her better. But halfway through the first session, I immediately knew it wasn't for me. Not only was the time commitment overwhelming, the format was also incompatible with my free-wheeling, rebellious nature. I tried to stick it out because I wanted to please my friend, but my heart wasn't in it. It wasn't long before I became a BSF dropout. The goal had become something that I didn't really care about.

Has this ever happened to you? You sign up for a 10K race or join a direct sales company, or you subscribe to a meal-planning program because your bestie is invested in it, not because you're committed to the project. It's really a secondary priority; your value is friendship or connection, so you may get swept up with their excitement or passion.

Unfortunately, second-hand motivation doesn't go far. It might get you off the starting line, but it won't get you through the tough spots. So if you are failing at your resolutions, examine if the goals are YOURS or someone else's.

Problem #3: We have too many goals at once. We have 47 resolutions for the year. We're going to lose 15 pounds, declutter our house, write 1000 words a day, and make our own soap. We're going to get up at five every morning to go to power yoga, and we're going to stop complaining, plant a garden, and finally – finally! – going to get serious about learning karate. Whew! I'm tired just thinking about it. But often that's exactly how we start off the year – with a list longer than our arm, delineating each and every goal we've ever considered. This is THE YEAR!

Until February. Then we're exhausted from trying to get up early, we're sick of washing with homemade soap, we weigh five pounds more than we did a month ago because we're stress eating, and we can barely walk from the power yoga classes. We've completely forgotten about the gardening and karate, and we never want to hear the word "declutter" again.

This is obviously an extreme, but it's not too far off the mark for many of us. We try to do too much, so we end up doing nothing. The solution is one we've already discussed: Do less to do more.

Once you address these three problems, there are some guidelines to creating goals that will get you on your way to changing your life – in a good way!

YOUR ASSIGNMENT: Have you ever fallen for any of these three goal-setting pitfalls? (If you're a people pleaser, #2 in particular should strike a chord of familiarity!)

CH. 10: GET SMART(Y)

If you've studied personal development, you may have heard of the phrase "SMART goals." SMART is an acronym which will help you set effective goals, and since we're all for effectiveness, let's review the acronym here:

S – SPECIFIC. As we've spoken about before, when setting goals you need to get rid of the vagueness. Instead of saying, "I want to get in shape," a specific goal would be, "I want to fit into my pre-pregnancy pants."

M – MEASURABLE. It's important to be able to track progress towards your goal, as well as to know when you've actually reached your destination. Selecting a goal that can be measured will ensure you know exactly how far you've come, and how far you have to go. So, rather than saying, "I want to save money," a measurable goal would be, "I want to save $5000."

A – ATTAINABLE. While I'm all in favor of selecting goals that take you outside your comfort zone and make you stretch, it's also essential to select goals you have a good probability of actually achieving. That means selecting something you have control over, and that is realistic. If you pick something completely outside the realm of possibility, such as that I, as a mid-forties, 5'4" female, want to play for the NBA, then the goal becomes demotivating rather than inspiring.

R – RELEVANT. A relevant goal is one that relates to your priorities. If you pick goals that aren't related to your priorities, it's no wonder you reach the end of the day or week and feel like you got nothing done, because you're not going in the right direction. Check to make sure your goal relates back to your priorities and will contribute to their achievement.

T – TIME-BOUND. Even if you have specific, measurable, achievable and relevant goals, if you don't set a time period, you won't be motivated to get moving. Many people set a 12-month goal, following the traditional year-long resolution cycle. But 12 months is a long time, and if you say you're going to lose 10 lbs. this year or save $5000, most people won't even start until September or October!

That's why I ask my coaching clients to set quarterly goals. You can have priorities that you've set for the year, but when we look at setting goals, we do so in 90-day chunks. 90 days is a perfect timeframe; it's long enough to see definite progress, but it's short enough to be very real. If you are going to accomplish something in three months, you'd better get started now because you have no time to spare!

While SMART goals are great, I expect more from you. You are a smarty-pants, so I want you to set SMARTY goals – with the last letter of course standing for a very important criterion:

Y – YOU CARE. You can set goals for your family, for your friends, for your kids, for your boss... but if you don't care about it, if it's not a SMARTY goal, I don't want to hear about it. You already do so much for the other people in your life. You already push off your own desires so often; I want to challenge you to select goals YOU care about.

YOUR ASSIGNMENT: For each priority you listed in the "First Things First" chapter, set one goal to accomplish in the next 90 days. Do not worry about these being perfect, or if this goal is what you really want. **This is a process**. Think of working through this book like going to cooking school – they may teach you how to use the deep fryer to make frogs' legs, something you'd never eat. But despite that, you're learning HOW to use the deep fryer. Then you can use it to make something you'd really want to make – like French fries!

Maybe you'll come up with more than one goal for each priority. Great! Just take five minutes or so and do it. Don't judge. We are in the no-judgment zone.

After you've listed your goals, go back and make sure each one fulfills the SMARTY requirements:

- Is this goal SPECIFIC?

- Is it MEASURABLE?

- Is it ATTAINABLE?

- Is it RELEVANT?

- Is it TIME-BOUND?

- Is it something YOU CARE ABOUT?

CH. 11: REDUCTION SEDUCTION

S MARTY goals are great – but they can still be too big! To translate them into something you can put on your to-do list, we need to reduce them, break them apart, until they're at a level you can actually get your minds – and your schedule – around.

Oftentimes if we make it past the "OLW" stage to an actual GOAL, we get hung up here. "Losing 20 lbs." is overwhelming... but drinking a green smoothie every morning? We can do that. "Growing closer to our family" is great, but fuzzy. We need to know what that looks like on a day-to-day basis. Does it mean eating together as a family three times a week, saying hello and goodbye, reading a bedtime story? We need to get to a level where we have tasks we can actually put on our to-do list.

ACTIONS → GOAL → PRIORITY

In reverse, we started with the priority, which led to a goal, which is now leading to actions.

It's critical to get that process down, because it's the key to creating powerful to-do lists. If we start with a goal that isn't related to a priority, we're going to feel lost. If we take actions with no clear goal in mind, we're going to feel like we're spinning our wheels. All three elements are needed to get us moving in the right direction.

YOUR ASSIGNMENT: In your own words, write out why each three of the elements is critical to successful progress.

CH. 12: THE POWER OF 15

I've got a superpower that I credit for my success. It is what has allowed me to build a multiple six-figure business, to move my family cross-country, to write books and to develop my coaching practice. It keeps me sane and balanced (as sane and balanced as possible, that is). And it's something you can use, too.

It's not leaping tall buildings, or X-ray vision, or even a golden lasso. What it is, is the ability to break projects down into tasks that can be accomplished in 15 minutes or less. Writing this book? It was done 15 minutes at a time. Creating classes and events? 15 minute chunks, baby. And speaking of babies, I used to say that if it didn't get done in the length of one "Barney" video, it wasn't getting done. Now that my kids are older and outside the big purple dinosaur range, apparently my attention span has dropped. 15 minutes is about all I can do at one time, but that's okay.

Sure, there are tasks that can take more than 15 minutes, like going to the dentist or hosting a webinar or attending a work meeting, but most (dare I say, 80 percent?) can be broken down to 15 minutes or less.

When I set out to accomplish a SMARTY goal, my next step is to brainstorm 15-minute tasks. I've gotten so good at this step that I often don't have to actually write them down because I know intuitively through experience what they are. Just as you don't have to write down your morning routine on your to-do list ("brush teeth," "shower," "put on pants"), I no longer have to break apart the steps involved in writing a blog post. I know it's going to involve 1. choosing a topic; 2. writing; 3. choosing a title; 4. finding a photo; 5. adding text to the photo; 6. publishing. I also know it will take me about two, 15-minute chunks to go through that process.

But at the beginning, it's imperative to write it all down. If you skip steps, you'll get stuck and you won't know why. You'll be tooling along and then all of the sudden, you'll come to a screeching halt, wondering why you aren't making progress anymore. Often it's because you've lost the path. You need to simplify and break things apart to the smallest discrete chunk and start again there.

You can make these project lists in a notebook of their own, or on a computer, but they DO NOT GO on your to-do list. I like to brainstorm in a blank spiral-bound notebook that I can refer back to (I have shelves of these books!).

There are tons of benefits from working in 15-minute chunks:

1. **It Circumvents Fear.** A lot of our goals – starting a business, writing a book, speaking in public – require stepping outside our comfort zone. And when we step outside our comfort zone, it requires risk. And risk means RESISTANCE[3] or FEAR.

2. It's only natural; we are hard-wired to avoid risk. Our nervous system kicks in. Our heart starts beating faster, our palms get clammy, and our stomach starts to roil. We didn't want to face the woolly mammoth, so our fear response is our body's way of telling us to get out of that situation, and fast.

3. But there's a big difference between facing the woolly mammoth and pushing "publish" on a blog post. Our brain tries to fool us into thinking that taking a tap-dance class is as risky as walking a tightrope across the Grand Canyon. Our thinking brain knows it's not true, but our emotional brain doesn't.

---

3   Steven Pressfield's book, "The War of Art," is a thorough and inspiring discussion of resistance. Read it, now! It will take only a few hours. And you can do it in 15-minute chunks! ;) http://www.lainloves.com/warofart

4. By breaking these scary tasks down, we can circumvent our emotional brains. We are acting at such a micro level that our ego doesn't get stirred up. We're not changing our lives... we're just drinking a green smoothie or picking up a brochure on becoming a personal trainer. It's like we tell our brain, "Nothing to see here, so move along!"

5. **It's Fast.** When we're working in 15-minute chunks, it's over and done with before we even know what's happening. We don't have time for our hackles to get raised; we're in and out, like a finely trained Special Forces squad. And even if the task requires us to muster our courage, we can see the end in sight before we even start. It's a lot easier to be brave when we know it's only for a limited time and we can see the finish line up ahead.

6. **No Brain Is Required.** We are so creative and talented that we can talk ourselves out of just about anything. If we have to choose whether or not we're going to participate in something, often we'll opt out – even if it's for our greater good. Just last night, I had intended to attend the Saturday evening session at our church because I had something to do this morning. But when the clock ticked closer and closer to my departure time, I came up with 110 reasons why I couldn't go. "I haven't taken a shower today." "I don't want to go by myself." "I can always listen on the podcast." I ended up not going – and I'm mad at myself!

7. If I *always* go to church on Saturday, then I don't think about it anymore. But since this was a one-time deal, it required thinking – and that brought back in the option to say "no." And so I did.

8. When we work from a pre-determined to-do list, we take the choice out. We don't allow our brain to come into it. It's

automatic, so we don't have the room to say "no." And by doing what we intend to do over and over, we create habits and routines.

9. Thinking also takes a lot of work! Knowing beforehand what we need to do takes half the work out of the process; then we just need to execute. Our brain uses one part to analyze and design a plan, and another part to execute. Think about having the general and the troops; the general designs the plan, and the troops execute without questioning the plan. When we move into execution mode, there's no time for your brain to jump in, or for resistance to spring up. By the time you realize what you're doing, you're done!

10. **It Compounds Over Time.** I tell coaching clients that they only have to work towards their goals for 15 minutes a day, most days of the week. You might be wondering how that little will ever make a difference. After all, these are likely goals that you've wanted to accomplish for months, if not years!

11. Remember our conversation about doing less to do more? That hinged on selecting the RIGHT things to do. It's true that 15 minutes might not sound like much, but we are talking about 15 minutes of concentrated, deliberate effort towards the RIGHT things. And over the course of a week that's an hour and a half (if we miss a day!) and over a whole quarter, that's over 20 hours! Imagine what you could get done in 20 hours!

12. When was the last time you had 20 hours free on your calendar? For me? NEVER. If I waited until I had 20 hours free before I started on a new goal, nothing would ever get done. But by breaking it down, I fit it in.

13. It's also important to note that if you DID have 20 hours set aside to work on your goal, it'd probably look something like

this:

14. 4.5 hours – "Getting ready" to work

15. 3 hours – Figuring out what to do next

16. 5.5 hours – Actual work

17. 2.5 hours – Deleting or undoing a good portion of what you did because you didn't think it was right

18. 4.5 hours – Checking in on Facebook to tell everyone that you are getting ready to work, working, undoing your work, or have just finished working

19. Contrast that with taking 15 minutes a day to do the next, right action, one after another, moving you forward a step at a time. You'll get a lot more done in less time.

20. **You Can Start Right Where You Are.** If you create your list properly, you'll be able to start RIGHT NOW. Because you plan out your to-do list beforehand, you know exactly what steps to take, in what order. You'll be in execution mode instead of wasting time figuring out what to do next. If you need a particular piece of information or tool or research before you can move forward, THAT becomes the next step.

21. NOTE: You may not know the ENTIRE list of tasks you need to complete, but you know the NEXT step, which is actually more useful. If you saw the full chain of tasks, you might get overwhelmed and never even start! By looking only at the next right step, you can focus your energy there and forget about everything else that needs to be done tomorrow, next week, next month.

22. **Everyone Has 15 Minutes.** Most of us don't have a spare 20 hours lying around, but we ALL have 15 minutes – even if we

have to break it into three sessions of 5 minutes, or we stay up late or get up early or miss 15 minutes of TV or Facebook. It's THERE.

23. Some days I have to take five minutes in the parking lot at the kids' school after I drop them off, then five minutes at lunch, and then my last five minutes while I'm cooking dinner (funny how everyone disappears when I start chopping onions! I could be selling all their possessions on eBay or downloading plans for building a rocket ship in the backyard, and they'd have no clue).

24. Like I said before, I won't make you give up hours of beauty rest or skip watching the last season of "New Girl" on Netflix, but if your big, wild dreams aren't enough to delay satisfaction for 15 minutes a day, maybe you'd better take another look at how committed you are to your priorities.

Are you now well and thoroughly convinced that a slim quarter of an hour can have you on the road to fame and fortune? Good. Let's test it out.

YOUR ASSIGNMENT: Pick one of the goals you laid out previously. Set your timer for 15 minutes (haha!) and make a list of 15-minute tasks to accomplish that goal. Don't worry about if they are in the proper order, or if the goal is your "best" goal. The best goal is one you can work on RIGHT NOW.

If you are stuck, ask yourself, "What's the very first thing I would have to do before I can reach my goal?" Keep asking that question over and over and write down those answers. Remember, this isn't the end-all, be-all. It's a working document that you can adjust and change over time as you discover more tasks that need to be completed, or you realize you can move forward without a particular step. This list is just your best effort as to what you see as the path for completing your goal.

If you are totally at a loss as to where to start, get some help! Find someone who has accomplished the goal before and find out what they did. For instance, if you want to lose weight and are thinking about the Paleo diet, you might want to check out online forums, get a book, or talk to a friend who's successfully lost weight using Paleo. That research becomes your first step.

NOTE: If you are thinking you need to "research," please refer to the section in the next chapter on the dangers of research. You can easily spend 15 minutes a day for WEEKS on "research." THIS WILL NOT HELP YOU CHANGE THE WORLD – OR YOUR LIFE!

CH. 13: ROCKING YOUR TO-DO LIST

We're almost there. We've laid the groundwork for our understanding of how our to-do lists must be based on our goals and our priorities. We've talked about what makes "SMARTY" goals. And we learned how to claim the superpower that will allow you to accomplish pretty much anything you want in your life. Now we're on the verge of learning how to create magical to-do lists. Give yourself a huge gold star for making it this far!

Before we take a look at your to-do list with new eyes, we have to talk more about one of the biggest pitfalls of productivity: The task vs. the project.

How many times have you written something like "organize house," or, "plan vacation" on your to do list, only to see it move from day to day to day on your list, until you figure you might as well get it tattooed on the back of your hand, because apparently it's gonna live with you until it's ready to move out and go to college – if that day ever comes? The frustration is real. Some part of you obviously wanted to accomplish this item because it made it onto the list, but why isn't it getting done?

A very simple answer. Because these types of items are not tasks; they are projects. And there's a big difference.

One pitfall I see over and over is the tendency to put PROJECTS rather than ACTIONS on our lists. We've discussed how it's critical to put only things you can "do" on your to-do list. That means we need to look at projects more critically.

The confusion of projects for tasks is one of the top mistakes I see people make with their to-do list. They write down things that are too large, that they can't "do." And then they wonder why those bigger life goals never get accomplished. It's simple: just like with your priorities, you have to take the big stuff and reduce it to a daily level.

Think about remodeling the kitchen. It's not something that you can put on your to-do list to "do." It's just too big! But you can break that project apart into steps to take, one after the other. For instance, you can call an architect, start a Pinterest board, call your friend and ask her what kind of refrigerator she has, talk with your significant other about budget, look into refinancing the house if necessary, etc.

Another, more familiar example: Making a cake. You don't just "make a cake." You measure out all the different ingredients, you stir them together in a particular order, you bake it for a certain period of time, you let it cool, you frost it, and then you can eat it. And even after that point, you then have to clean up the kitchen (or convince one of your kids to do it, which might be a project in and of itself!).

Every project that you want to accomplish, every goal and dream on your life list, must be broken down into its individual parts. If you don't approach them in the right order, the cake doesn't turn out right. This principle will be one of the biggest lessons you learn as we go through these next sections on creating and using your own to-do list.

This step is particularly critical when working on life-changing goals. I noticed when working with my clients that their bigger goals are often secret hopes and dreams and even bucket list items that they hold dear in their hearts, but never really seem to get done.

When I would dig a little deeper into why people weren't working towards these goals if they were their heart's desire, I discovered a few things. First, people were scared. And I don't blame them! If I had something on my to-do list like "write best-selling novel," I wouldn't dare tackle it either! It is too darn intimidating, and I can't control the outcome.

With big projects like this, there's also no entry place. If I'm staring at a to-do like "change the world," it's like staring at Mount Kilimanjaro without seeing a path up. I don't know about you, but I would not start hiking without a map, a plan, and a huge pack full of essentials – and the International Search and Rescue on speed dial. I would need to know where to start, where others have gone before, and where I can set my pack without it falling into a crevasse. Breaking projects apart into tasks provides this path for you. Just like climbing a mountain, you're not going to know each and every single footstep, but you do know the general direction you're heading. And having that direction makes all the difference.

Let's say I'm working with a client, Bess, whose priority is to end world hunger, and Bess decides that in the next 90 days her goal is to write a 1500-word article on the prevalence of hunger in the world, and present three high-level ideas for addressing hunger.

Remember our recipe example above? Bess then imagines this large goal (writing the article) as a recipe for a particularly scrumptious cake. Bess knows that, as we discussed earlier, each cake has to be broken up into its ingredients and its appropriate steps. These steps are the tasks that she is going to put on her to-do list. And she needs to be able to accomplish each one in 15 minutes or less. So...

"end world hunger" → "write article on world hunger and propose ideas" → list of 15-minute actions

BESS'S LIST OF 15-MINUTE ACTIONS

1. Research statistics on world hunger.

2. Find the names of three experts on world hunger.

3-5. Look up contact information for each of the three experts.

6. Compose email to expert asking if she can contact them for a phone interview to gather information.

Etc.

Obviously, that's not a complete list. There will be many other steps that arise as Bess moves through just these first six actions. Her list might become 100 or even 1000 items long – but by taking each one in turn and focusing on it until it's completed, she keeps her big priorities in sight while moving forward to her goals. If she discovers another step to take, she just writes it on the project list where she thinks it goes. If she gets completely stuck, she asks herself, "What do I need to know or do RIGHT NOW before I can take the next step?"

Another fictional but very awesome client, Cori, says her priority is helping people have healthier relationships. Her goal is to write a book to share her knowledge. She thinks that she can have the background information and angle completed, and the first three chapters of her book written, in the next 90 days.

"Better relationships" → "write book" → list of 15 minute actions

CORI'S LIST OF 15-MINUTE ACTIONS:

1. Make a list of possible topics for a book.

2. Do an Amazon search for viability of topics.

3. Choose a topic.

4. Brainstorm angle.

5. Outline contents.

6. Write for 15 minutes.

7. Repeat step number six as many times as necessary.

Again, there's a lot more to writing a book than these seven steps... but this gives Cori a great outline to start from... AND she can start with the first one right now, today. In just a week she could be on her way to writing, and in 90 days she could be well into her manuscript! Every day, she gets a bit closer to her goal of helping others through her book.

When we are tackling big projects, we need a clear plan and a clear starting place. By putting the next right step action on our to-do list, we ensure it's something we can tackle, and can tackle today. While looking up the phone number for the local chiropractic school so you can inquire about classes may not seem like a big step towards getting your degree, it is the first step. And you can't take any subsequent steps until you take that first one.

If the first step is too big for you, you'll never even try. By breaking it apart into tiny pieces, though, each individual step seems do-able – almost too much so! – and when you tackle them, you experience success over and over again. You've heard all the platitudes: "The journey of 1000 miles begins with a single step," and "How do you eat an elephant? One bite at a time." They are platitudes for a reason. They are platitudes because they are true.

Small actions taken consistently over time lead to big results. While writing this book, I received this email from one of my coaching clients, Allyson, who had been having trouble making progress on her dream of launching an online business: "I wanted to tell you that the calendar system you recommended is working AWESOME. I got a blank calendar and at the end of each day, I write what I did for my new business in the box. Some days I am crazy exhausted but I still pick at least one 15-minute thing because I refuse to break the chain!"

Allyson is going to make her dreams happen. Maybe not in a week or even a month, but it will happen. Why? Because of her consistent actions in the right direction, 15 minutes at a time. That's all it takes.

DANGER, WILL ROBINSON! or, THE PROBLEM WITH RESEARCH: Research can suck up tons of time and resources and make us feel like we are moving forward without getting anything tangible done. If you need to "research" before taking the next step, limit your research to – you got it! – 15 minutes. If you find yourself taking more than 15 minutes, you've fallen into analysis paralysis. The solution is to TAKE ACTION. If you read three blog posts on the best baby stroller to buy and ask three friends what they suggest and you get no consensus, they're probably ALL reasonable options. Don't allow research to be an excuse for staying stuck. If all else fails, flip a coin.

YOUR ASSIGNMENT: Before I ask you to get started on your own goals and projects, let's try another fictional one, just to test the waters and make sure you've got the hang of this.

Let's take a fictional, yet very lovely and accomplished, client named Stephanie. Stephanie's priority is to become debt-free, and her goal for the next 90 days is to pay off her lowest credit card balance. Please complete the following, suggesting 15-minute actions for Stephanie's goal. Remember, it doesn't have to be in order, or complete. Just lay out a general plan for her to follow. After you've listed at least five 15-minute actions, make note of which item(s) you think she could start with, right now.

"Become debt-free" → _____ → fifteen-minute actions

STEPHANIE'S 15-MINUTE ACTIONS

1.

2.

3.

4.

5.

CH. 14: SLASH AND BURN

With my own business and a few very active kids, you can imagine that my to-do list is pretty lengthy – probably much like yours. I often pride myself on how much I can get done. But several years ago, I ended up on bedrest for two months (it's a long story). During that time, I was feeling really lousy and had very little energy, to the point where I could accomplish about one thing a day. I learned very fast what the critical elements were in order to keep my business and my family moving forward.

During that eight-week period, I eliminated a ton of items from my list, I delegated a lot, and I focused on the 20 percent (or less) that was critical. No, the kitchen didn't get cleaned to "mom" standards. No, my business didn't grow in some areas because I simply didn't have the time to devote to marketing. I didn't read as much as I normally do. Facebook had to move on without me. No, I didn't get my hair cut, or go shopping for new clothes, or even shopping for groceries. But you know what? Things held steady. My family survived, my business survived, and I came out the other side with a new realization of the 80-20 rule, as I saw very clearly what was essential and what was busy work.

One of the most compelling promises I made to you is that you can do LESS to do MORE. And in this section we're going to dive right in with our machetes and flamethrowers to totally rip your to-do list apart. At the end of this chapter, you're going to see how it is possible to find not only one, but several 15-minute segments throughout your day that you can designate for your goals and priorities. Let's talk about how four simple questions can help you remove the majority of these problems.

As much as we talk about "making time," we know that we can't manufacture more hours in the day. We can reallocate hours and minutes from one category or task to another, but we're all dealing with the same 168 hours per week. So to "make time" for your most important tasks, what we really need to do is remove the stuff that doesn't matter or matters less, so we can reallocate that time to a higher-priority area.

When people come to me with cram-jammed to-do lists containing enough to keep Beyonce's staff busy for a week, let alone a single 24-hour period, I tell them to get out their list and a red pen, and ask themselves the following four questions:

1. **Does this have to be done?** (What would happen if this didn't get finished? Can I live with that?)

2. **Does it have to be done by me?** (Can I outsource, hire someone else, get the kids to do it, swap tasks with someone...?)

3. **Does it have to be done now?** (Can it be delayed to next week, next month, next year? What would happen? Can I live with that?)

4. **Do I enjoy doing it?** (If I HATE it, go back through the three questions... push yourself.)

When I first introduce these questions, there's typically some automatic pushback. The idea that some – if not most – of the items on your to-do list are unnecessary isn't a pleasant one. After all, you've been spending your energy, your lifeblood, on these tasks, and to take a good, hard look at them and say you've simply been wasting your time is a rude awakening.

I liken it to when I went on a decluttering binge before moving cross-country. I went into my closet and saw the clothing I'd spent good money on but never worn, and the shoes I'd taken from their boxes maybe once or twice, and the baseball caps and scarves and other accessories I'd purchased with every intent of wearing – but which instead had just ended up as clutter in my home. Then I saw the books I'd bought and never read, the yarn I'd fallen in love with but never turned into a hand-knit project, the kitchen utensils that remained unused... you get the picture. The amount of money I'd spent on unnecessary items was simply staggering, and it made me literally sick to my stomach.

The same can be true when we look at where we're spending our time. Three hours a week spent on mixed-doubles tennis when you (a) hate tennis and (b) end up fighting with your husband? That's time better spent elsewhere. Two hours a month at the networking group you outgrew last year, but still feel obligated to attend? Three hours a month at the book club when you haven't ever enjoyed the assigned book, or the discussion? It's time, my friend. Don't look back and tally up all the "wasted" time; instead look forward and vow to make some changes. We can't change what's already happened, but we can change what we allow to continue.

When you start asking yourself these questions, you're going to opt for the path of least resistance. OF COURSE you have to be the one to deliver the donuts on teacher in-service day (and they should, obviously, be home-baked as well). OF COURSE someone has to mulch the flowerbeds THIS WEEKEND – and no one does it quite like you do. Of course.

But what is the cost? If you are spending four hours baking and delivering donuts, what are you NOT doing? If you are spending the weekend mulching the flowerbeds, what goals are you NOT achieving?

I'm going to get tough with you for a minute. We operate under the delusion that time is limitless, and we can always fit in "one more" thing. But each hour you spend watching "Dancing with the Stars," or babysitting your next-door neighbor's niece's kittens, or doing your co-worker's report because she didn't do it and it has to get done, is an hour you do not have available for your own goals and priorities.

Now, I'm not going to tell you to eliminate all those things from your life. In fact, we've already talked about how I *want* you to have time for relaxation and fun. But I also want you to realize that everything you choose to do has an opportunity cost. You've probably been telling yourself for years that you can fit it all in – but you're not. And YOUR goals and priorities are the ones that are suffering.

I'm also not trying to take everything off your to-do list so all you have left to do is sit around the swimming pool, watching the cabana boy and drinking mai tais, but I do want to remove enough stuff so you have the time to accomplish what you've already said are the driving forces in your life. That means freeing up 30-60 minutes a day, most days.

Let's take a look at a sample "to-do" list with about 30 items. I compiled this with help from my Facebook community, so it represents real tasks from real people just like you. It's chock-full of stuff that represents projects versus tasks, non-essentials, and busywork. Plus, if Lulu (our fictional heroine) were to try to accomplish all these items, it would take a month, not a day!

We're not going to dive into whether the items reflect goals and priorities at this point; we're just going to do a quick weed-through to remove anything that doesn't meet the four criteria above. Our goal is to get the list down to a manageable, reasonable (for today) level:

LULU'S "TO-DO" LIST (BEFORE)

1. Sort through magazines

2. Paint stairwell

3. Take out trash

4. Paint the house

5. Purge closet/clothing

6. Organize photos

7. Move furniture

8. Do three loads of laundry

9. Sell clothes on the swap site

10. Compile a list of people who still need a photo taken for a project for the youth soccer league

11. Trip to Costco

12. Go to Hobby Lobby or Staples for that new thing I want

13. Gather son's laundry/empty dishwasher

14. Cook dinner from scratch

15. Check out latest online class

16. Go for walk

17. Get photos off husband's computer so I can finish 2015 scrapbooking project

18. Work on my Amazon Prime Watch List

19. Collect all my recipes and put into Word documents

20. Putting craft projects up for sale

21. Organize files for taxes

22. Take the cans and bottles to the recycling station

23. Call my mom

24. Organize the craft room

25. Digitize all my photos and transfer all digital photos to backup

26. Request medical records from doctor

Now let's have Lulu ask herself these four questions (*Does this have to be done? Does this have to be done by me? Does it have to be done today? Do I enjoy doing it?*). Here's here end result with her (my fictional) commentary:

1. ~~Sort through magazines~~ *This doesn't have to be done at all, or I can leave it for later.*

2. **Paint stairwell** *This stays – we're getting ready to sell the house, and we have the paint. It's a two-person job, so my husband and I will do this right before bedtime tonight. It should take about an hour, and we have all the supplies we need.*

3. ~~Take out trash~~ *This needs to be done, but my son can – and should! – do it.*

4. ~~Paint the house~~ *Needs to be done, but we're not ready. It's a project, not a task.*

5. ~~Purge closet/clothing~~ *Doesn't need to be done TODAY.*

6. ~~Organize photos~~ *UGH. This has been on my list forever, and I could outsource it to one of my kids, or start working on it at a craft night with some friends. It's not linked to any particular priority, other than it is something that needs to be*

done SOMEDAY. Plus, it's a project, so I'm crossing it off.

7. **Move furniture** *I am going to enlist my husband's and son's help so we can get this done quickly. It has to be done today so we can have access to the stairway.*

8. **Do three loads of laundry** *I could outsource this to one of the kids, and that's a long-term goal, but it requires training them... so for today, it stays. We have no clean underwear!*

9. ~~**Sell clothes on the swap site**~~ *I should just give them to the shelter, but I am currently using the thought of making money by selling them as a way to not have to let them go. It sounds ridiculous when I read it back. I'm just going to donate them.*

10. ~~**Compile a list of people who still need a photo taken for a project for the youth soccer league**~~ *This isn't the first step. Instead, I should simply send out an email to the department and ask people to let me know if they still need their picture taken. That will take 3 minutes instead of 30.*

11. ~~**Trip to Costco**~~ *Doesn't have to be done today. I also could make a list and ask my husband to go.*

12. ~~**Go to Hobby Lobby or Staples for that new thing I want**~~ *Ummm... I'm being honest. This is not essential.*

13. ~~**Gather son's laundry/empty dishwasher**~~ *These are his chores but I do them most of the time because it's easier than bugging him to do it. I'm not going to do them today!*

14. ~~**Cook dinner from scratch**~~ *I love to cook, but I could pull out a freezer meal that I've prepped*

15. ~~**Check out latest online class**~~ *But I waaaaannnt toooo! Haha!*

16. **Go for walk** *As much as I'd like to outsource this, health is a priority. And I can call my mom (#23) while I'm walking!*

17. ~~**Get photos off my husband's computer so I can finish 2015 scrapbooking project**~~ *I can ask him to do this. He used to do this every week but I started doing it. Also, it's not something that needs to be done today.*

18. ~~**Work on my Amazon Prime Watch List**~~ *I laugh seeing it say "work." This is totally for fun and non-essential.*

19. ~~**Collect all my recipes and put into Word documents**~~ *This is not essential today, and I could also outsource it. And if it never got done? I'd live.*

20. ~~**Put craft projects up for sale**~~ *I'd love to do this someday, but it's not the "next step." And it's not necessary while we are trying to get the house ready for our move!*

21. ~~**Organize files for taxes**~~ *This is also a project. I've been avoiding it, pushing it from one day to the next. I want to dive in today so I am making progress a bit at a time instead of scrambling on April 12, trying to pull it all together. I'm going to remove this item and break it down more.*

22. **Spend 15 minutes sorting receipts into months** *Ah, much better!*

23. ~~**Take the cans and bottles to the recycling station**~~ *This doesn't need to be done at all. I will probably get no more than $10 bucks for almost an hour of work! I should just put them out by the curb for pick-up.*

24. ~~**Organize the craft room**~~ *The rest of the house needs more attention, and I get very distracted in the craft room. Plus, most of my supplies will end up getting boxed up for the*

move, *so I don't even need to organize it until it's unpacked on the other end.*

25. **Call my mom** *This is a must-do. Relationships are a priority for me, and I'm committed to talking to my parents at least once a week.*

26. ~~**Digitize all my photos and transfer all digital photos to backup**~~ *See the comment above on organizing my photos! This is definitely something I want to do someday, but that day is not today. And I could outsource this.*

27. **Request medical records from doctor** *I could outsource this and it could be pushed off to tomorrow, but it's one of those things that may take time for them to pull together, so I'm going to bite the bullet and to it today. I've already looked up the phone number and put it in my planner. It'll take five minutes (hopefully!).*

28. **Send out email to the league to ask who needs to have their picture taken** *Ah, much easier!*

LULU'S TO-DO LIST (AFTER)

1. Paint stairwell

2. Move furniture

3. Do three loads of laundry

4. Go for walk

5. Spend 15 minutes sorting receipts by month for taxes

6. Call my mom

7. Request medical records from doctor

8. Send out email to the league to ask who needs to have their picture taken

Lulu's unmanageable so-called "to-do" list has been reduced to a very manageable seven items that are completely do-able in a day's time. And by removing all the extraneous items (most of which she wasn't going to get to anyway), she's given herself breathing room.

What would have happened if she hadn't asked herself the critical four questions? She'd likely be sitting in her favorite chair, flipping through magazines to "sort" them, or she'd be out buying more stuff from Costco or Staples that she'd then have to organize.

Some of the other items will still get completed with help from others, and some items she'll tackle in the future when it becomes a priority. The point is not to push things off indefinitely, but to practice "just in time scheduling." It means we don't fill our schedule with projects that are unnecessary; we get to them when we need to, not when we're using them as an excuse to tackle other things. Sometimes these items can also be batched to save time – like spending three hours one Saturday a month to make freezer meals that we then eat throughout the month.

If you're still unclear or the four questions are getting confusing, let's make it easy. Each time you are faced with a choice, I want you to ask yourself:

Is This the Highest and Best Use of My Time?[4]

Knowing our time is limited on this earth as well as on a day-to-day basis, we have to make choices. We're making choices already, each time we push the activities related to our goals to the next page of our calendar. This process simply brings those choices front and center.

---

4   To download an artistic rendition of this quote to print or use as a screensaver, please visit the book bonus page at http://www.lainehmann.com/rytdlextras

YOUR ASSIGNMENT: Go through a recent to-do list, asking yourself the four questions. Try to remove at least 20 percent of the items on your list. If you are really struggling, pretend you just threw out your back and have to go on bedrest for the next week. What items can be delegated, pushed off, or left undone completely? Who could you ask to help you?

CH. 15: DO AS I SAY...

A t this point, you've got the knowledge you need to rock your to-do list, and rock it good! You know how goals, priorities, and 15-minute tasks are related. You've seen why it's critical to break apart projects into sub-tasks and tasks. You've learned how to free up time for your higher purposes, and you are equipped to avoid many of the biggest productivity pitfalls, AND you've heard all my worst jokes. So since we're now besties, I thought it would be helpful to walk you through my own priorities and how I translate them from priority to goal to tasks.

I'm in a unique position in my life with my first child about ready to go off to college. As a result of the coming changes to our household, right now, family takes the number-one priority spot. And since I have to pay for that college education, finances are in a close second, followed (always) by fitness. I have several others, but to keep things simple, I'm going to focus on those top three.

My Priorities

1. Family

2. Finances

3. Fitness

Based on those priorities, I set the following goals for the next 90 days:

FAMILY: Create small scrapbook for Ben with pictures and memories from his 18th birthday Facebook post.

FINANCES: Eliminate $500 in unnecessary monthly expenses, and save that money instead.

FITNESS: Run a half-marathon that I've signed up for next month.

You'll see that each goal is "SMARTY:" specific, measurable, attainable, relevant, time-bound, and one I care about.

Let's look now specifically at the family priority:

"family" → create small scrapbook for Ben → 15-minute actions

MY 15-MINUTE ACTIONS:

1. Find pictures from each year of his life. (this will likely take 45 minutes, so three sessions).

2. Upload pictures to Shutterfly and order

3. Make list of supplies I'll need to complete the album

4. Order any needed supplies

5. Assemble supplies in box so I can pull it out and put it away

6. Crop photos to fit

7. Trim papers to fit

8. Write memories (probably will take an hour, so four sessions)

9. Assemble book (probably take an hour, so four sessions)

After the tasks are laid out, I can see that I'll need about four hours, or 17 sessions of 15 minutes each, to complete this goal over the next 12 weeks. That makes it really easy to determine how many days per week I'll need to dedicate to this project. Because I've done several similar projects, I am pretty certain that my time estimates are correct. If this were a project I weren't quite as sure about, I could build in extra time to make sure I'm on track.

The next step would be to actually schedule the time in on my calendar, whether it will be one session of an hour a week, or several shorter sessions. I can also determine if I want to work on specific days, or just keep my weekly goals in mind. Whatever I decide to do, I have all the information I need to make sure I meet my deadline. I now have no excuses – and I'm super-excited about this project!

YOUR ASSIGNMENT: Revisit your priorities and goals and choose one to break apart in this manner. Choose one that you feel relatively confident about, and comfortable with. Then, based on your time estimates, slot your working periods into your calendar.

CH. 16: TROUBLESHOOTING

Refer to this section of top five to-do list problems when your list isn't "working." Use it to diagnose your to-do list issues and figure out how to treat them.

#1: Too Much on the List.

The problem: You have more on your list than you could ever accomplish.

The symptom: You feel overwhelmed and like a failure because you're never getting "enough" done.

The cure: A to-do list should contain only items that you can realistically accomplish TODAY.

#2: Not Specific Enough.

The problem: The tasks are vague, or you're not sure what they mean.

The symptom: You look at your list but aren't sure where to start or what to do first, so you skip over some big-ticket items that would truly affect your life, and instead go after the easy tasks you intuitively understand.

The cure: Write down the task with enough specificity to take immediate action. If you're missing information or tools, THOSE are the next steps.

#3: You Write Down Projects Instead of Tasks.

The problem: You write down items that can't be "done" in one sitting.

The symptom: Your list never seems to change, and you never seem to make progress on your biggest goals.

The cure: Break larger projects into smaller sub-goals and tasks, and add only items that take less than 15 minutes to your list.

#4: Your List Contains Items Not Related to Your Biggest Priorities.

The problem: Your list contains items you are not committed to, or that reflect older or outdated priorities.

The symptom: You move through your list with a sense of detachment or lack of enthusiasm, or you skip items because they bring no joy to you.

The cure: Start with priorities, move to SMARTY goals, and then – and only then! – add items to your to-do list.

#5: You Write Things Down but Then Don't Do Them.

The problem: You aren't doing the stuff you've claimed you need to do.

The symptom: The 20 percent items keep getting pushed from day to day as you do the 80 percent of items that aren't truly moving you forward.

The cure: Break down these tasks as small as possible. Instead of "write for 15 minutes," try, "write for 3 minutes."

The cure #2: STOP THINKING. Take the emotion out of the tasks. Instead of looking for excuses and telling yourself how much you don't want to write or make the phone call or go to the gym. Stop making it an option. Just execute.

YOUR ASSIGNMENT: Bookmark this page to refer to when you start to struggle. Help is only a page away!

CH. 17: FAQs

You've got questions, I get that! This is a lot of information to digest, and as I stated early on, everyone's list, priorities, goals, and life is different. Here are some of the most common questions I hear:

What if I can't finish everything on my list every day?

I'm going to say something here that may make you gasp in horror, swallow your gum, and/or throw this book across the room. You should be finishing everything on your to-do list every day.

With the RYTDL approach, you're only going to write down things you really care about, things you could complete during that specific day, and items that can be done in one sitting of (usually) 15 minutes or less. If you follow those guidelines, let me repeat: there is no reason you should not be completing 90+ percent of the items on your list.

Sure stuff happens. Kids get sick, unexpected opportunities arise, the car breaks down or runs out of gas… I'm not talking about those days. Although, if those days are more your normal then the exception, that's something else we need to take a look at.

If you're consistently finishing only half or less of your list, there is one of two problems:

1. You're overestimating the time you have, or

2. You're underestimating how long it takes to complete tasks.

If you're overestimating the time you have to complete your list, you need to examine your daily schedule. If you are homeschooling your six kids, spending three hours a day designing websites, and managing the family farm, it's going to be unrealistic to expect to accomplish an additional six or seven hours' worth of work. Get a daily schedule laid out in 15 minute increments, and block out everything that's already accounted for – sleep, meals, commute time, work outside the home. Then see what you have left. THAT is what you have to work with; if it's five hours or 30 minutes, you need to trim your list to fit.

If you're underestimating how long it takes to complete tasks, you're not alone. In my book, "FOUND: Rediscovering Your Dreams, Your Voice, and Your Life in 15 Minutes a Day," I talked about our human propensity to project that tasks we dislike will take much longer than they really will, while those we enjoy, we think will take less time than they actually do. It's sort of like underestimating the calories in a donut, while overestimating the calories in asparagus. They're just about the same, we tell ourselves, so we might as well have the donut!

Sometimes we actually do not know how long certain tasks will take, but over time, we'll figure it out with more precision.

In either case, the solution is to keep a time diary. Download the free time diary tracking sheets from the resource section at the end of this book, and keep track of what you're doing, how long you think it will take, and how long it actually took, for AT LEAST one week. Over time, you'll get much clearer on what you can accomplish in any given time period.

This is all well and good, but I have a list full of other people's priorities and assignments, and they won't let me remove anything. Help!

Typically, this is a boundary issue. I truly believe that we train people how to treat us, so if your family is expecting you to do all the household tasks, deliver a hot lunch to them at work or school, run all the errands, and put yourself last, always, this is behavior you are tolerating. Slavery was outlawed in the 1800s, so it's time to remind them – and more importantly, yourself – that you have the right to say "No."

The process of removing yourself from obligations is not an easy one. It requires getting very clear on what you want to accomplish in this lifetime, and then being willing to withstand the momentary discomfort of telling others you are no longer going to do the things they've always counted on you to do. Let me repeat, this is not easy, but it is straightforward. You have 24 hours in the day; how many are you going to dedicate to other people? What is reasonable to reserve for yourself?

The answer to those questions depends on you, the stage of life you are in, and the other people you are committed to. I suggest working with a trusted friend, counselor, or coach to help you find the strength and the words to remove yourself from tasks, projects, and commitments that do not meet your personal priorities.

There's all this stuff on my list that I don't want to do, but I can't outsource or put off. Stuff like going to the dentist, or finances, or asking people to help with a high-priority project I'm working on.

Go back again and see if there is any way you can outsource some of these tasks. You may not be able to hire a full-time bookkeeper, but can you hire a high school student to sort your receipts and prep them for data entry? Can you trade "assistant" services with a friend, where she makes some phone calls for you as your "assistant," and you perform some less-odious task for her? Get creative.

Sometimes you do have to just suck it up and finish it. And if that's the case, use the process of breaking it down into smaller pieces to remove the large, negative feelings that may be associated with the larger goal. One project I'm always putting off is my taxes. As a self-employed professional with several income streams, it can get really ugly, and I hate doing it! But when I start thinking about it in steps – "sort receipts by month," "make a list of missing statements," etc. – it gets a lot easier. I remove the big ugly "TAXES" project and replace it with much more pleasant simple steps.

Rewards can work really well, too! Promise yourself a trip to Starbucks after you finish your phone calls, give yourself permission to watch a Netflix show after you finish your phone calls. But make sure you eat the veggies before you head for dessert! That's part of being a grownup.

I've tried all your suggestions, but there are still items on my list that keep getting pushed off. I don't understand why. They're not too difficult, but I don't ever seem to get them done.

I've had this very issue myself. About a year ago, I had a series of phone calls I needed to make. Although I dislike calling people on the phone, I knew the calls weren't a big deal, but I just couldn't seem to get them done. They'd get pushed from day to day, and it was starting to cause issues as some important personal projects weren't getting finished.

When I took a minute to ask myself very clearly why I kept skipping these items, I realized that I usually reserve my out-and-about time for phone calls – while driving to pick up the kids from school (on my headset, of course!), or while I'm waiting in the parking lot at soccer practice. At the start of the day, I'd skip the calls because I'd intend to do them later. But when "later" came, I'd skip the items for a very simple reason – I hadn't written down the phone numbers!

When I'm working through my list, I'm completely in execution mode. Anything that causes me to delay gets skipped, and I'll move on to the next task. I'm not thinking – I'm getting as much done in a given amount of time as possible. If anything requires further research or is unclear, I'm not stopping. Because I didn't have all the information needed to complete the task, I simply skipped it.

The solution was obvious, and it worked! By writing down the phone number next to the notation, "Call doctor," I'd actually DO it. I had skipped a step because it was so small, I didn't think it mattered. But it did.

So if you are skipping items for no apparent reason, the "next step" you've written down may not be the real next step. For instance, if you find that you haven't made a phone call you need to make, the next step is to LOOK UP THE NUMBER. If you need to order a new tire for your car, make sure you know what size and brand. Have all the information you need to execute without delay.

How many goals is too many?

How many kids is too many? I've seen some people who seem tapped out with one, while a good friend of mine makes having triplet boys and a girl seem easy! Depending on your personality, schedule, and other demands on your time, you may be able to handle three or four goals simultaneously – or you may need to focus on one at a time. Start out with one 90-day goal for each of three of your priorities, and see how that works. You can cut back or add more as needed.

I have several priorities with a 90-day goal in each. How do I balance those goals? Do I work on each of them every day?

Once again, the answer to this question depends on what's happening in your life, your personality, and your goals. Some people find they are more productive when they work on just one goal at a time, focusing all their spare time and effort on it. Others (like me!) like to work on several goals at once, moving between them.

What I've discovered is that there is always downtime for any goal. When I was training for my half-marathon, there were days where I wasn't scheduled to run. On those days, I could use that "running" time for pursuing other goals.

I'm constantly writing a book – like this one! And while I love to write, there are days where I just can't spend five more minutes at the computer. On those days, I work on one of my other goals, like my son's scrapbook album. On other days, I might work on all three or four of my goals. It depends on my schedule, my energy level, and where I am in the project list.

You can also work on goals in serial – one after another. For instance, I finished my half-marathon last weekend, so that goal is completed for this 90-day period. But instead of taking off the next 70 days, I've got another fitness goal of starting a weekly yoga class. That goal kicked in as soon as the first goal was accomplished.

Play around with your goals. As long as you are making consistent progress, it matters less that you work every day than if you are moving forward.

I keep jumping from goal to goal. I can't seem to settle down on anything! As a result, I am not making progress and feel really scattered.

Perfectionism can cause us to look for the "perfect" goal, the one that will make the biggest impact as you work to align your life with your priorities. But let me tell you a dirty little secret:

THERE IS NO "PERFECT" GOAL. PERFECTION DOES NOT EXIST!

The "best" goal is one you can take action on, right now. Let's face it; there's no way to know if Goal A will be "better" or "worse" than Goals B, C, and D. And what does "better" even mean? Instead, think of the process as experimentation. Start with a goal and tell yourself you cannot switch for 90 days. This is also where a coach or accountability partner can be very helpful. They can help hold you to your stated goals, and help you bust through any obstacles or doubts you might have. Don't try to go it alone!

Okay, I committed to three goals for 90 days, I'm working towards them most days, but I'm scared I'm not going to reach my goals. What then?

Fear can really do a number on us! It makes us think that it's better to not try, rather than try and "fail." But failure is also deceptive; what if I trained for my half-marathon but had to walk partway? Or I was sick the day of the race and couldn't finish it? Well, some people might think that's a failure, but instead, I would have told myself that success came in the preparation.

What if your goal was to have family dinner three nights a week, but you only managed two on average?

What if you wanted to lose 15 lbs. but you only lost 12?

What if you wanted to save $1000 but you only saved $999?

What if you wanted to write 100 pages in your book but only finished 80?

We get so focused on the finish line that we forget that goals are accomplished in the process – and that as long as we are moving forward, we are MOVING FORWARD.

There are no Goal Police who will publicly shame you for only losing 12 lbs. There is no jail for individuals who don't finish their books by a self-imposed deadline. There is no penalty for missing the mark by 10 percent, 20 percent, or more.

You are a success because of the habits you are creating. You are a success for what you have done. You are a success because you promised yourself you were going to do something and you did it.

I love this quote. I looked for the author, but couldn't find it, so if you know, send me an email! Heck, maybe I made it up myself:

"However slow you are, you are still lapping everyone sitting on the couch."

However long it takes you to run the half-marathon...

However long it takes you to save $1000...

However long it takes you to write your book...

...You are still faster than everyone who didn't try.

YOU ARE CREATING A POWERFUL FUTURE WITH EVERY ACTION YOU TAKE.

RESOURCES

Eat That Frog by Brian Tracy

The War of Art by Steven Pressfield

FOUND: Rediscovering Your Dreams, Your Voice, and Your Life in 15 Minutes a Day by Lain Ehmann

Free video from me

Time Diary Worksheet

ABOUT THE AUTHOR

After building my online business to six figures in only 18 months, I began coaching other women to do the same. But through my business coaching I discovered that knowing WHAT to do was only part of the battle; the bigger challenge was helping my clients believe that they COULD have the business – and the life – of their dreams. While I still do a bit of business coaching, I've shifted my focus to helping women find their unique voice amidst the cacophony of family, friends, societal demands, and expectations.

I offer a variety of coaching programs, from monthly group coaching to one-on-one sessions, through which I help women live their lives LOUD, sharing their gifts and talents with the world, and holding nothing back!

With degrees from Stanford University and Syracuse University, and decades in the professional and entrepreneurial world, I love finding innovative and unexpected solutions to life's challenges and problems. My gift is sorting through the overwhelm of information, ideas, expectations, and noise to find the simple path that leads back to YOU.

You can find out more about me and my programs at
www.lainehmann.com.

41577497R00065

Made in the USA
San Bernardino, CA
16 November 2016